Tarot cards
Crystals and
spells & witches brew.

This book is dedicated to my loving and wonderful family.
My husband Roderick, and my children Gracelyn and Greyson. May you always follow God's plan for your life without fear.

Copyright   2023   Jaylin Monroe

All rights reserved solely by the author. No part of this book may be reproduced, distributed, or transmitted in any form or by any means, or stored in a database or retrieval system without the prior written permission of the author.

ISBN: 979-8-850957-56-8

Can witches get into heaven?

Jaylin Monroe
Author and Illustrator

In the city of Sorcerer's Haven, there was young girl named Imani. She was tall with curly hair which made her look a little funny.

It was a cool Friday afternoon and the day of her family's ritual fest. The town liked when the sun disappeared and the moon put on its nighttime best.

This year, Imani was asked to make her grandma's famous witches brew. She was nervous and didn't like the pressure from her family's crew.

To get the ingredients for the potion, she went to the apothecary. There she found all she needed to make the brew quite scary.

When she walked toward checkout, someone's book fell on the floor. Imani picked it up to hand to them, but they quickly ran out the door.

She looked down and read aloud, the words on the cover. My notes from The Holy Bible. "Hmmmm, what have I discovered?"

Imani was so curious about the words she saw.

She kept the book, made her purchase, and left the store in awe.

She came to a crossroads and decided to go a different way than before.

Imani's mind was filled with thought as she walked out of the store.

As she walked, she asked herself, "Why do I feel this way?" There must be something more to this, but let me get through this day.

Finally home, Imani rushed to her room. She grabbed the book to read. She opened it up and felt something sharp and quick like lightning speed.

She turned to the very first page and saw it was labeled, number eleven. It said,

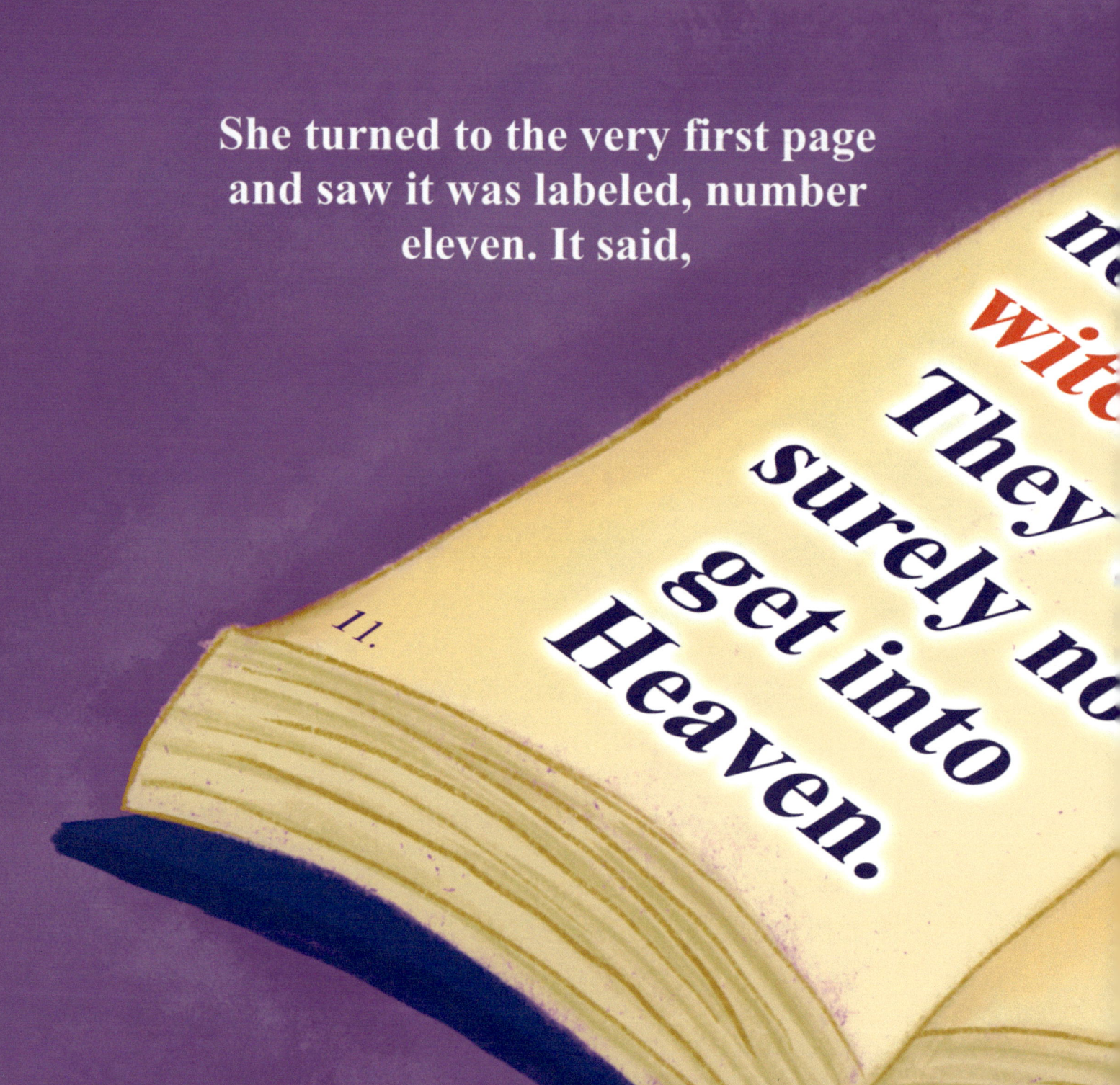

Imani started to question everything she believed. All of it was being blown away like the wind carrying leaves.

MAGIC
FEAR
PRIDE
TRADITION
SAGE
CONTROL
CRYSTALS
EVIL
SPELLS

After the festival and the day had ended, Imani was ready to lay down for a rest. She jumped in her bed and laid still, hoping to wake up refreshed.

She fell into a deep sleep and dreamed of a man named Jesus. The she thought, "I've heard of him. He's the one who frees us."

"You are my beloved daughter," Imani could clearly hear. "Trust me. Come to me. You have no reason to fear."

As the sun peeked through the curtain, Imani quickly awakes. She falls to her knees and confesses her sins and all of her past mistakes.

Her room flooded with light. The birds outside her room flew. Imani, undone by her dream, cried out, "Jesus, Jesus, I love you."

LOVE ♥ ♫ peace
patience ☆ joy ♪ hop
gentleness self-cont
faithfulness ☆

Imani will never forget that dream and how Jesus led her to freedom. She has much more to learn and now she can do it in His Kingdom.

Tarot cards
Crystals and
spells & witches brew.

HOLY BIBLE

Release that stuff for Jesus, the one, who saved you.

Made in the USA
Columbia, SC
15 April 2024